GEOGRAPHY ENCYCLOPEDIA

BIOSPHERE

Om Books International

Contents

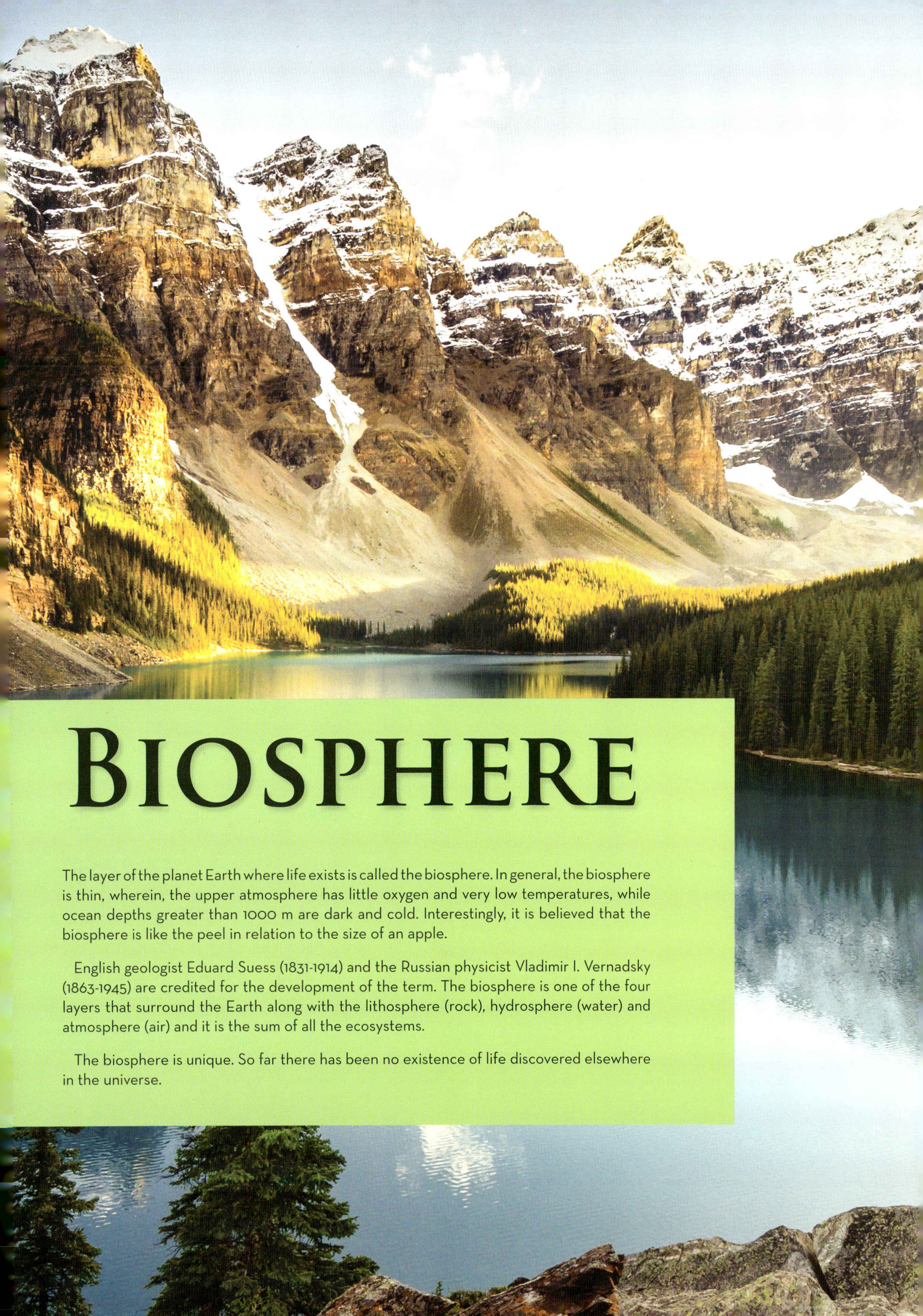

BIOSPHERE

The layer of the planet Earth where life exists is called the biosphere. In general, the biosphere is thin, wherein, the upper atmosphere has little oxygen and very low temperatures, while ocean depths greater than 1000 m are dark and cold. Interestingly, it is believed that the biosphere is like the peel in relation to the size of an apple.

English geologist Eduard Suess (1831-1914) and the Russian physicist Vladimir I. Vernadsky (1863-1945) are credited for the development of the term. The biosphere is one of the four layers that surround the Earth along with the lithosphere (rock), hydrosphere (water) and atmosphere (air) and it is the sum of all the ecosystems.

The biosphere is unique. So far there has been no existence of life discovered elsewhere in the universe.

PLAINS

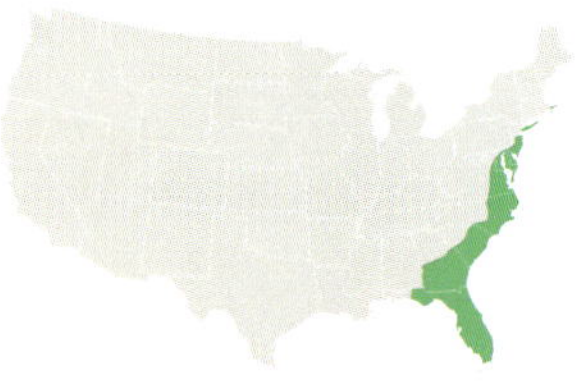

Sometimes, sediments are deposited by the flowing rivers that pass along the valley of a mountain or plateau. As the river flows, its force widens the floor of the valley. These can also result in the formation of a river plain. There are three types of river plains—floodplains, alluvial plains and coastal plains.

Floodplains

Melting snow or heavy rains cause some rivers to flood with excess water. These flowing rivers then deposit the mud, silt and sand on the surrounding banks and landscapes instead of carrying it downstream. The sediments of these deposits collect over a period of thousands of years and form plains. Such plains are called floodplains. The plains at the banks of Onon river in Mongolia are an excellent example of floodplains.

A floodplain in the Isle of Wight.

Coastal plains

The flat lands that separate oceans from mountains or plateaus are called coastal plains. These coastal plains can sometimes be the result of sediments that are deposited from rivers that flow towards the seas. The Atlantic Coastal Plain is one of the world's largest coastal plains.

Alluvial plains

When rivers flow from the valleys of mountains onto level landforms, the sediments that are carried by the river flow out onto their banks as well as the surrounding landforms. These sediments are deposited in a level manner on the land and, over time, this forms an alluvial plain. The plain formed by the Waimakariri River in New Zealand is a suitable example of the alluvial plain.

Example of an alluvial plain.

A plain formed from glacial deposits in Iceland.

Glacial plains

While the movement of rivers causes the formation of alluvial or floodplains, the movement of ice in colder regions forms glacial plains. The glaciers on land move slowly and cause erosion in the areas in which they pass. As they move, they deposit sediments of gravel, sand, silt, clay and marl. These sediments are also formed by the melting of glaciers. Over time, these sediments are deposited to form glacial plains. Such glacial plains are called "outwash plains". True glacial plains are those formed by pure glacial matter such as marl. Deposits of marl are also collected to create cement and fertilisers. The Kankakee Outwash Plain is an example of a glacial plain.

THE GREEN HABITAT

A forest is a habitat that is home to hundreds of species of trees, plants, animals and insects. Forests have been around for nearly 400 million years. The world is a mix of old and young forests. All forests are covered with trees that grow near each other. Forests are limited to areas that experience regular rainfall as trees cannot grow tall and dense without it.

History of forests

Forests came into existence nearly 420 million years ago. During this time, ancient plant species (now extinct) slowly developed and began to cover the land. These plants adapted to the many changes in their surroundings for the next millions of years. The early forests saw tall ferns that had a height of 40 feet. These forests also had lots of moss and shrubs.

It was only about 140 million years ago that flowering trees and plants first appeared on Earth. These trees evolved and also contributed to the evolution of the animals, insects and birds that lived here.

Moss, shrubs and trees cover the soil of the forests.

Terminology

These common words describe forests and their features:

- **Emergent or upperstory:** the uppermost layer of trees that receive plenty of sunlight.
- **Canopy:** below the emergent layer of the closely standing forest trees that cover the ground completely. The branches and trees of most forests are right at the top in order to receive adequate sunlight.
- **Understory:** these are short trees, covered by the canopy. They require little sunlight and plenty of shade.
- **Forest floor:** this is the floor or land of the forest consisting of the topmost layer of the soil, leaf litter and other waste.
- **Ground cover:** it consists of fungi, mosses, wildflowers, ferns, small plants and shrubs that cover the ground. These only appear in forests whose canopies leave some opening for the sunlight to reach the forest floor.

Pleistocene Ice Ages

During this time, Earth's forest cover was occupied by tropical forests. Temperate forests began to develop as a result of the climatic changes. These were followed by the boreal or taiga forests. Today, nearly one-third of Earth's surface is covered by forests. 70 per cent of the carbon (existing in all living things) is accounted for in the forests.

TROPICAL RAINFORESTS

Forests can be classified in different ways. Most forests are classified according to the climatic zones in which they lie and the types of trees that grow within the forest. By this classification, the forests of the world can be classified as tropical rainforests, temperate rainforests, temperate deciduous forests, temperate coniferous forests and boreal or taiga forests.

Lush and evergreen

Forests that receive lots of rainfall through the course of a year are called "rainforests". Tropical rainforests lie close to the equator and lie within the tropical zone (+23.5° N to –23.5° S). They are among the oldest ecosystems on Earth. Though only 6 per cent of Earth's surface is occupied by tropical rainforests, nearly half the world's plant and animal species are found here.

A type of fungi growing in the tropical rainforest.

Soils

As the climate is hot and humid throughout the year, the soils of the rainforests decompose dead organic matter at a fast rate. This allows the fungi and roots of trees and plants to quickly absorb the nutrients made available by the decomposition process. So, the soils lose their fertility.

The high and continuous rainfall keeps the soil wet and soggy for most parts of the year. The heavy rainfall takes away nutrients from the soils so that some areas have soils that are low in nutrients. Chemical and physical weathering of soils also rocks and soils is faster here due to the warm climate.

Climate

Tropical rainforests experience a hot and humid climate. One of the main features of tropical rainforests is that they do not experience winter. They have a dry or monsoon climate. Daylight lasts for 12 hours followed by 12 hours of night. The average temperature remains high at 20-25°C and this rarely changes. During the winter or summer seasons, the temperature may fall or rise by a margin of 5°C. Tropical rainforests have an annual rainfall of 200 cm or above.

Animals

Different animals live at the different layers of the tropical rainforests. Tropical rainforests have four layers that are divided based on how much sunlight each layer receives. The first is the emergent layer which receives the maximum sunlight. Trees of the evergreen forests grow as tall as 200 feet. They have strong, hard wood with trunks that have a diameter of 16 feet. The leaves of these trees are broad. The tops of these trees form the emergent layers. Eagles, monkeys and bats along with various species of butterflies, live in this layer.

Tree frogs and snakes are some types of fauna that live in the canopy layer.

Animals at the canopy

The canopy layer is much thicker and provides more cover than the emergent layer. A majority of the tree animals such as snakes, tree frogs and toucans live here as there is lots of food and shelter. Sunlight is abundant here.

Further classifications of evergreen forests

Evergreen forests are further classified into different types based on the seasons they experience. These classifications are:

- **Evergreen rainforests:** These forests experience rainfall throughout the year. The plants do not go dormant. These forests do not experience a cold or dry season.
- **Seasonal rainforests:** These experience very short dry seasons. During this time, the trees experience minor changes in appearance due to the drop in the levels of humidity. However, the rest of the time they experience the same climate as evergreen rainforests.
- **Semi-evergreen rainforests:** These forests experience longer dry seasons so that the emergent trees are deciduous while the understory trees are evergreen.

FUN FACT

Tropical rainforests are considered to be "self-watering" forests. The water absorbed by plants is later released into the air due to the sun's heat. Each canopy of these forests can annually release about 760 litres of water!

Problems caused by human beings

One-half of the tropical rainforest cover has been destroyed due to human activities. In the past, human beings have destroyed these forests through deforestation and forest fires in order to clear the land to construct roads, develop agricultural farms or to build houses.

Animals at the Understory

The understory layer gets little sunlight. The trees have larger branches and leaves that extend upwards to catch sunlight. Leopards, jaguars and other species of tree frogs live here. Almost 90 per cent of the insect population of rainforests is here. As it is completely dark in the forest floor, only decomposers and bacteria live here. There are also ground animals like anteaters.

TEMPERATE FORESTS

Temperate forests are located in the temperate zones. As we go towards the Polar Regions, these forests include deciduous and coniferous trees. Based on climate and vegetation, temperate forests are further classified as evergreen and deciduous.

A cardinal.

Climatic changes

The average temperature in a temperate forest is -30 °C to 30 °C. The day-to-day weather experiences sudden and fast changes. During winter, the temperatures can drop very low. As we go towards the Polar Regions, the temperatures can drop to freezing points. The vegetation is therefore greatly affected by these changes in temperatures.

During the winter season, the days in the temperate forests are very short while the nights are long. The leaves of the various plants and trees become damaged by these freezing temperatures. Some leaves even stop functioning, thus affecting the process of photosynthesis.

Leaf shedding

The forests located to the east of the USA, west of Europe and in China, Japan, Russia and Canada also experience these sudden drops in temperatures during winter. However, the soils in these forests are rich in nutrients and moisture. Here, the trees have been able to adapt to the climatic changes.

These trees have thin and delicate leaves that have a very short lifespan which lasts for one winter season. At the end of the season and towards autumn, the plants shed their leaves. They begin to have leaves again in the spring. These leaves are called "deciduous" and forests that have such leaves are called "deciduous forests".

The trees of a forest shedding their leaves in autumn.

Seasons

Temperate forests receive precipitation continuously through the year while falls as snow or rain as per the season. During the spring and summer, the precipitation falls as rain while, during autumn and winter, it falls as snow. Temperate deciduous forests receive an annual rainfall of 75–155 cm.

Flora and fauna

Deciduous trees that shed their leaves such as the maple, birch and oak trees, are a major vegetation here. Various species of ferns, wildflowers and mosses grow on the forest floor. They also have a mix of coniferous and evergreen trees such as fir and pine. The animals adapt to long, cold winters and sudden weather changes. These include the woodpeckers, cardinals, hawks, etc.

A red-tailed fox.

Temperate forest cover with ice in winter.

A Cedar tree.

Coniferous trees

These forests are also called "coniferous forests" as they have many coniferous trees. The soils are rich and have a thick upper layer of decomposed organic matter. The trees grow tall and are supported by plenty of rainfall and mild weather. Coniferous trees such as pine, Douglas fir, redwood, cypress and cedar dominate this vegetation. There are also some deciduous trees present.

FUN FACT

The weather in the temperate forests is so unpredictable, that the people here have a saying, "If you don't like the weather, wait a minute".

Temperate evergreen forests

The areas of the temperate zone that receive heavy and regular rainfall and experience mild and pleasant winters (such as the coastal and mountainous regions) have temperate evergreen forests. Salmon, marmots, black bears, spotted owls and deer are some of the commonly seen animals of this region.

New Zealand, the southern parts of Japan, and some parts of Europe and Canada have temperate evergreen forests. The climate and weather here remain stable with negligible change in temperatures. These forests have high precipitation that ranges from 130 cm to 500 cm.

A yellow-bellied marmot.

Threat to temperate forests

Some parts of temperate deciduous forests receive acid rains as a result of the harmful emissions from vehicles and industries. This acid rain acts upon the leaves to weaken their resistance and damage them. After a prolonged exposure to acid rains, trees in the temperate deciduous forests have been producing fewer seeds.

On the other hand, both temperate deciduous and temperate evergreen forests are growing thinner and weaker due to climatic changes. Deforestation, mining, construction of roads and other unregulated human activities are posing a threat to the existence of these forests. Today, only some parts of the original temperate forests are scattered across the globe.

Aerial view of deforestation.

BOREAL FORESTS

Boreal forests are also referred to as "taiga", which is a Russian word meaning "forest". These forests are spread out in large bands across the North American and Eurasian continents in a near-continuous, uninterrupted line. Boreal forests are limited to the Northern Hemisphere. These forests also lie to the south of the Arctic Circle.

Vegetation

Boreal forests have dense canopies created by evergreen trees. Spruce, needleleaf, pine, fir and other coniferous and evergreen trees dominate the vegetation of these forests. There are also some deciduous trees. There are very few species of the trees that make up these forests, among which the fir and spruce species are the majorly seen trees. The thick canopy allows very little sunlight to reach the understory, so there are few species of trees here.

Pine trees are traditionally used as Christmas trees.

Furry animals

Animals with thick coats of fur are found here. These animals include moose, caribou, wolves, wolverines, grizzly bears, hares and some species of deer.

Animals of the boreal forests, such as the grizzly bear and wolverine, are mostly carnivorous.

Location

Boreal forests are located between 50° and 60° latitudes in the Northern Hemisphere. Today, the world's biggest taiga (boreal) forest is located in Russia. It is 5,800 km wide. Parts of Canada, Alaska, Siberia and Scandinavia also have boreal forests.

Soil

The decomposition of dead organic matter takes a very long time as the temperature and upper layers of the soils are cool. The soil here is thin when compared to the soils of tropical and temperate forests. It is low in nutrients and fertility, and is also acidic.

Climate

Boreal forests have longer winters than summers. These forests receive an annual precipitation of 40-100 cm per year, which falls to the ground as snow. These forests constantly experience low temperatures. Compared to the temperate and tropical forests, boreal forests receive very little heat, energy and light from the Sun.

DRY AND MONTANE TROPICAL FORESTS

The tropical forests lie within the tropical zones of India. They are further classified as dry tropical and montane subtropical forests. "Montane" refers to something that occupies mountainous land. Dry tropical forests are further classified as dry deciduous, thorny and dry evergreen forests based on the trees they are made up of.

Broad-leaved forests

These forests are classified under the montane subtropical forests. They are located in the Silent Valley, Western Ghats and Eastern Himalayan range. Evergreen trees are the dominant trees of this region. There are also scatterings of deciduous trees. Oak, birch, cherry and chestnut trees along with bamboo, orchids and creepers are found here.

Pine and dry evergreen forests

The forests have tall trees with many dry, shiny leaves. They appear buffed and glossy on first glance. These forests experience long, dry and hot seasons followed by a short, cold winter. Pomegranate, oleander and olive trees are some of the trees found here.

Dry evergreen forests are located in the Shivalik Hills along with pine forests. Western and Central Himalayas, and the Manipuri Hills have pine forests. Pine trees such as oak, pine, rhododendron and amla dominate this forest.

Flowering rhododendron and pomegranate plants.

A flowering bamboo tree.

Dry tropical forests

Dry deciduous forests are found in the north, west and southern states of India such as Gujarat, Andhra Pradesh, Madhya Pradesh, Karnataka and Tamil Nadu. These forests are dominated by the sal, bamboo and acacia trees that form canopies of 25 m.

Thorn forests have rich, black soil. They are found in all parts of India except in the east and northeast. These trees grow about 10 m in height. Cactus and spurge are typical trees of this forest type.

Dry evergreen forests are located in the coast of Karnataka and Andhra Pradesh. There are some deciduous trees that cover the land, but mostly there are evergreen trees with broad, strong leaves and colourful, fragrant flowers.

Temperate and Alpine Forests

Montane temperate forests, that is, temperate forests on the mountains of India, are also classified as wet, moist and dry forests based on the climate and types of trees found here.

The forest surrounding the Nilgiri hills.

Wet montane forests

Wet montane forests are located to the north and south of India. They are found in the states of Kerala and Nilgiri Hills in the South and in Arunachal Pradesh in the north. These forests receive an annual rainfall of 200 cm. They are located 1,800-3,000 m above sea level. The forests in the north are much denser than those in the south.

Another speciality of the forests in the north is that they have three layers. The first layer, which is the highest, has coniferous trees while the second has deciduous trees. The last layer has champa and rhododendron.

Moist and dry montane forests

The Western and Eastern Himalayas have moist forests. However, Eastern Himalayan ranges receive more rainfall, so they have thicker and more lush forests. These forests contain a mix of evergreen and coniferous trees.

Sikkim, Kinnaur, Lahul and the neighbouring areas of the Himalayas have dry forests. These forests have coniferous trees such as ash, maple and oak. As we go higher up the mountains, we can see the chilgoza and deodar trees.

Alpine and subalpine forests

Alpine forests are those that are located on high mountains. The Myanmar Hills and the Himalayan mountain range are the main places where Alpine forests are located. They are covered with tall and thick evergreen trees, and rhododendron and birch. The forest floor has patches of ferns and mosses. Moist Alpine forests receive lots of snow. Dry Alpine forests are found 3,000-4,900 m above sea level. They are covered with small or "dwarf plants" such as juniper, willow and honeysuckle.

Subalpine forests are situated on the higher slopes of mountains, but below the tree line. The subalpine forests of India are located in Kashmir and Arunachal Pradesh and in parts of Western Himalayas. The vegetation is similar to that of Alpine forests.

BOTANICAL AMPHIBIANS

Mangrove forests are one of the most important forests of the world, but are also the most threatened. They grow on the edge of rainforests, where the sea meets rainforests. Some parts of the vegetation grow on land while some grow in water. This is why mangroves are considered to be "botanical amphibians".

Aerial view of a mangrove forest and the open sea.

Location

Mangrove forests are composed of mangrove trees and plants. "Mangrove" is a fern, shrub, palm or tree that grows in a tropical or subtropical climate, close to the equator. It cannot exist in cold temperatures.

They grow above sea level, within intertidal zones or estuaries of coastal areas. They cover 39 million acres. They are concentrated along tropical ocean coasts.

What is an "intertidal zone"?

An intertidal zone is an area where land and sea meet. They are found in estuaries and bays as well as on sandy beaches and rocky shorelines. High tides and low tides come to rest in the intertidal zones.

An intertidal zone.

Aerial and tap roots

Mangrove trees appear to be standing on water with the help of stilts. This is because their roots are visible above the ground. They are called "aerial roots". These roots are thick and tangled around them. They keep the leaves and trunks of trees on the surface of water and above the waterline. These trees also have tap roots.

The trees experience some movement by the rise and fall of tides. Mangroves experience regular floods as a result of the water from the tides. They are controlled by roots. The tides and roots control where sediments from the soil will settle and form a muddy layer on the surface. Together, the aerial and tap roots filter the salt in water and provide the right amount of nutrients to plants.

Mangrove roots.

Mangroves under threat

There are about 80 species of mangrove trees that grow in these forests. The widest range of species is found in the mangrove forests of Australia. Mangrove forests are important to maintain the marine ecology of any area. However, they are under a lot of threat. Only 50 per cent of the original mangrove forests now remain on Earth.

NATURE'S FACTORY

Forests are very important for our existence. They are one of the reasons this Earth is habitable by humans. Forests are packed with life such as plants and animals and it all grows on the lifeless soil. Some forests have been in existence since hundreds or thousands of years.

Wood harvesting.

Raw materials

The forest is also called "nature's factory". We get many raw materials from forests such as fruits, paper and wood. We use them to make books, medicines, houses, furniture, cleaning powders and cosmetic products. A majority of the nutritious soil on Earth was once formed in the forests. It is like another raw material where the end product is the trees and plants of the forests.

Commercial value

Forests have many plants and trees that are useful not only to produce raw materials but also have ornamental value. There are many organic and homeopathy medicines that grow in the forests. Various nut trees, sal, sandalwood and ebony trees are of high commercial value as well.

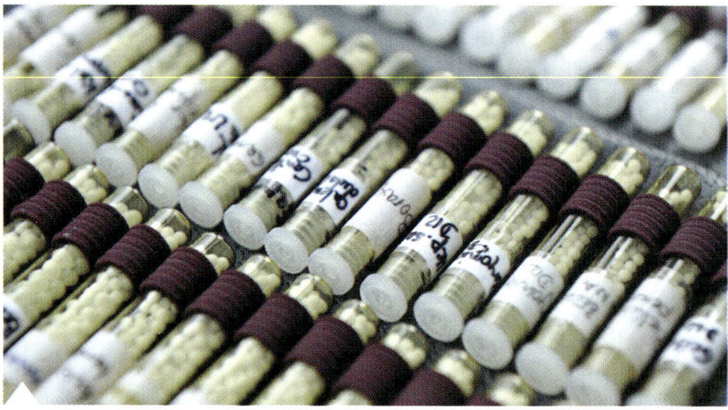

Homeopathy medicines sold commercially in the market.

Soil

The forest is like a soil-producing factory. The many trees and plants of forests hold soil in place during storms, heavy rains and winds so that very little weathering and erosion takes place. This keeps the soil rich and retains its properties for a long time. If all the forests in the world are cleared away, the soils will be eroded at a very fast rate.

Water

Rainwater or flowing river water is stored in leaves, roots and soils. During heavy rains, trees also hold water in trunks and branches. This water is stored away for later use. The trees of the forest control the speed and direction in which the rivers flow. If the trees didn't hold water, the plants would die due to its shortage. Forests also help bring rain to the land through the "water cycle".

NATURE'S HARSH SIDE

Earth is a place of extreme climatic differences. At one and the same time, one end of Earth might feel hot while some might feel cold. The hottest weather is experienced at the equator where maximum rays of the Sun fall directly upon Earth's surface. The coldest weather is experienced towards the poles where there are very little sun rays that fall upon Earth's surface. The deserts are one of the hottest places on Earth while the Polar Regions are the coldest.

Desert temperatures cool as the sun sets.

What is a desert?

When people think of deserts, they immediately think of words like "hot", "barren" and "sand". There is very little precipitation in the desert areas. The annual precipitation in most deserts is about 25 cm. During the day, deserts can be as hot as 50°C. Many deserts have cold nights and extremely cold winters. Deserts are tough but still habitable. People have been living in deserts for thousands of years.

The cold desert

Antarctica is the coldest place on Earth. About 98 per cent of the Antarctic continent is covered with snow. This is greater than the entire USA. This is why Antarctica is also called the "cold desert". Antarctica has few species of moss and lichens that live upon the surface of rocks.

Polar Regions

The Arctic has a population of millions of people. However, conditions in the Antarctic are difficult and mostly uninhabitable, so it has no permanent population. Cold, harsh winds blow across these regions. Standing here for even a minute without wearing protective clothes (such as thick sweaters and thermal innerwear) is impossible. Here, winter seemingly lasts forever. The temperatures drop to negative degrees.

Pictures of these regions might make it seem like there is no vegetation here, just a thick coat of snow and ice. However, many different species of plants and animals live in the Polar Regions. These species also exist under water. Over many years, they have adapted to adjust to the harsh never-ending winter of the Polar Regions.

A polar bear on ice.

NATURE'S GREEN CARPET

Grasslands are commonly found in all continents of the world except Antarctica. They are open and comparatively flat lands that cover about a quarter of Earth's surface. As the name suggests, there is an abundance of grass in the grasslands and this is how the plains are easily characterised and distinguished as grasslands. They are classified as tropical grasslands and temperate grasslands based on the climatic zone within which they fall.

Suitable climate for grasslands

Grasslands are not completely arid and barren like the desert lands and nor do they receive high rainfall like forests. Grasslands experience a relatively dry climate with low and irregular rainfall. The rainfall received is about 20-100 cm per year.

Grasslands lie within the temperature and subtropical zones. Due to the low rainfall, the only vegetation that can grow in abundance is grass. The climatic conditions do not allow for the growth of taller plains or shrubs. Usually, grasslands lie between forests and deserts and are considered transition lands.

A picturesque grassland in Kansas, Texas, USA.

Temperate grasslands

Shrubs and trees are completely absent in temperate grasslands. The amount of annual rainfall is comparatively lesser. The height of the grass is dependent on the rainfall received by the grassland. For example, areas that receive heavier rainfall have taller grasses. Grasses are the main vegetation found in temperate grasslands. The pampas, veldts and steppes are examples of temperate grasslands.

The soil in temperate grasslands is of a darker colour and has deeper layers. The upper layers of the soil are more fertile and rich in nutrients as the roots of the grasses are deep and have many branches. Temperate grasslands have hot summers, where the temperature rises to about 38 °C and cold winters with temperatures that are as low as -40 °C.

A landscape from the temperate grasslands.

FUN FACT

The grassland plants keep growing despite being cut down or eaten by humans and animals. This is because the growing parts of the plants are located near or under the soil.

Eroded valleys

Some rivers run along valleys. Over time, sections of these valleys are eroded into broad, flat lands. This is why plains exist between mountains or plateaus. These are called "erosional plains". The sediments and particles carried from the valleys are sometimes deposited within a sea or an ocean. These deposits of sediments gradually build to a great height and rise above the sea level. The result is what we call a "coastal plain". These plains are very fertile and highly suitable for agriculture.

Changing appearance

Based on the climate, the grasses and grass-like plants undergo a change in appearance. In dry climates such as winter or fall, the grasses appear dull and lifeless. During the spring season, flowers appear on the grass-like plants in temperate and tropical grasslands. But the surrounding grass remains dull and brownish in colour. With the onset of the monsoon season, the grasses and grass-like plants regain their green colour to look livelier and richer.

A tropical grassland in Africa.

Bright fall in a prairies field.

Tropical grasslands

Tropical grasslands are mainly found in Africa, Australia, South America and India. As they are largely found in Africa, they are also called, "savannah". Tropical grasslands develop in areas with about 50-127 cm of annual rainfall. However, the rainfall in these areas have to last for about 6-8 months in a year, with droughts in the remaining months.

Artificial grasslands

Many grasslands that were earlier considered to be natural are now being categorised as artificial grasslands. It is believed that a long time ago, people burned down the forests and vegetation that grew in certain dry places to create these artificial grasslands. A majority of the grasslands on Earth are considered to be artificial or maintained by artificial procedures.

Names around the world

Grasslands have different names around the world. In North America, grasslands are called "prairies", while in South America, they are called "pampas". In South Africa, they are called "veldt" while in Central Africa, they are called "savannah". In Central Eurasian countries such as Russia, grasslands are called "steppes" while in Australia, they are called "downs".

CHANGING THE FACE OF EARTH

Humans make use of raw materials and fertile soils from forests by cutting down trees and clearing land. The materials from trees are used to produce various goods. The land is either used to build houses or as a farm to cultivate crops. Over a period of many years, the forests have been cleared without consideration for the future. The main culprit is money.

Agriculture

Since the invention of agriculture, about 50 per cent of Earth's forest cover has been destroyed. Agriculture is the most important cause for deforestation. Forests are cut down to make room for farms and pastures. Farmers then plant crops and graze their livestock here. Some farmers also cut down small acres of forests for personal use. Here, they grow crops that will feed and clothe their families. This agricultural practice is called "slash and burn".

Forests are sometimes cut down to create tea plantations.

Illegal practices

Forests are cleared to make room for roads and increase connectivity in transportation. They are cleared to reach more remote areas where there are taller and beneficial trees. This is monitored and regulated by the government. However, some members of logging industries illegally cut down forests to make a profit.

Deforestation is done for agriculture or the use of wood. Once a forest is cleared, people benefit by selling the goods acquired or selling the deforested land.

Illegal logging is common in Madagascar.

FUN FACT

Deforestation takes place on a large scale all around the world. It has been estimated that every year we lose forest cover the size of Panama.

Wood harvesting

Wood harvesting, also called "logging", refers to the practice of clearing forests to acquire wood. This wood is sent to various industries that use them as raw materials. Wood is used to make paper, build houses, make furniture and is also used as fuel in charcoal industries and houses.

How can we stop deforestation?

The obvious solution is to stop clearing forests. However, this is not possible as we need raw materials and agricultural land. However, we can reduce the area that is cleared per year. The materials we get from forests can also be used carefully and smartly so that there is less need to cut down more forests. The method can be rethought so deforestation happens in a way that does not greatly damage the ecosystem. Forests that are cleared can slowly be replaced by planting new trees.

Afforestation is replanting a forest one seed at a time.

Climatic changes

A major and most concerning result of deforestation is the changing climate. Earth has become hotter and hotter in the past 50 years. Trees absorb greenhouse gases which affect global warming. With an ever-reducing forest cover, there are fewer trees. This means that more greenhouse gases are able to enter the atmosphere. This has increased the effects of global warming.

Slash and burn

Slash and burn is carried out by burning farms. Farmers might intend to burn down only a small portion of the farm. In a lot of these cases, the fires have gotten out of control, leading to a much larger area getting destroyed. This mostly destroys the understory layer. If these still-burning trees fall to the ground, they damage the forest floor and destroy the plant growth there.

Unintentional deforestation

Deforestation is sometimes indirectly carried out on a small scale. Natural fires and the overgrazing by animals which stops new growth are also some of the reasons for deforestation. Deforestation of a small part of the forest breaks the continuous canopy layer. More sunlight reaches the ground and with enough intensity, starts a natural fire that damages the forest floor.

LIFE IN THE GRASSLANDS

Many animals live in the grasslands. The animals of temperate grasslands are not as diverse as those of the tropical grasslands. Most animals of the grasslands are herbivores, which means they feed on plants and grasses. There are also some carnivores and omnivores.

Animals of the tropical grasslands

The fires experienced during this time chase birds, animals and insects away from their settlements. Insects may die out during the fires. The bigger animals and birds run or fly away to safety. Small animals that build burrows underground (such as rabbits), go underground and do not return until it is safe.

There are many herbivores in the tropical grasslands, such as rabbits, elephants, giraffes, horses and zebras. They live comfortably during the wet and rainy monsoon seasons. However, they experience a shortage of water during the drier climates. The surface water is absorbed by the soils and there is a lot of competition between animals, insects and birds for water. So, most birds and some large land animals migrate to another place.

Animals of the temperate grasslands

Foxes, falcons, antelopes, elephants, giraffes, bison and coyotes are some animals of the temperate grasslands. Smaller animals such as ground squirrels, badgers, prairie dogs and gophers also live in these grasslands along with various birds and insects. The major birds of the temperate grasslands are turkeys and eagles.

At one time, there used to be millions of bison that resided in the North American prairies. Towards the 1800s, early European settlers hunted them down for food, textile and game. Now we see very few bison in the wild. Bison is mostly bred by humans in commercial herds.

Conversion of grasslands

Grasslands thrive on repeated disturbances such as fires or grazing. The dead organic matter at the surface gets cleared out and makes way for new growth. If this matter settles on the surface for too long, it would prevent nutrients from reaching the roots and shoots of plants. Thus, human and animal interactions help maintain and recycle grasslands.

Bison at the prairies.

Effects of humans on grassland

The climatic conditions and the land of grasslands is ideal for agriculture. Grasslands have rich, deep soil support and provide nutrition to various types of crops. As a result, a majority of the natural grasslands on Earth have been converted to agricultural farms. Now, instead of native grasses, we see more of commercial crops. The animals, birds and insects of grasslands are forced to move away as well. Overgrazing by cattle and sheep slowly destroys the soil and natural vegetation of a grassland.

VEGETATION OF THE TROPICAL GRASSLANDS

Grasslands are said to have originated during the Eocene. The Eocene is the name given to a period of time that started about 56 million years ago and ended 33 million years ago. The major grasslands of the Northern and Southern Hemispheres came into existence due to the dry and arid climate of these places. It is believed that the first humans (that appeared in Africa), occupied the savannahs.

Changes to climate

Grass first began to grow in the tropical savannahs nearly 50 million years ago. Prior to this, the climate underwent slow changes such as a decline in the amount of rainfall experienced by this region. The climatic conditions slowly became dry and arid. Savannahs first began to develop in Africa, Australia, the southern parts of Asia and the tropical portions of America.

Soils and other vegetation

Soils of the savannah provide little nutrition and fertility. The nutrients lie at the surface of the soil where organic matter decays at a speedy rate due to the hot and dry climate. The soils are rich in iron and, therefore, appear red in colour.

Trees and shrubs are sparse and spread out widely. Very few areas have a covering (called "canopy") of trees that shelter the grasses from fire, drought or animals. Trees are only found in areas with deep and rich soils. Deciduous trees are the most commonly found trees here. There may be shrubs that cover certain parts of the savannah land.

Vegetation of the tropical grasslands

The major vegetation of tropical grasslands is the various species of perennial grasses that grow here. Lemon grass, star grass, Bermuda grass and Rhodes grass are the major species of grasses that cover this area.

Forbs grow alongside grasses. They have small, broad leaves. Different types of grasses compete for space in the tropical grasslands. Usually, there are only one or two major types of grasses covering large stretches of land. For example, the grasslands of the Serengeti plains are dominated by the Rhodes grass.

A close-up of the Rhodes grass.

VEGETATION OF THE TEMPERATE GRASSLANDS

Temperate grasslands are called by different names based on the country in which they are located. The temperate grasslands of Russia are called "steppes" while those of Argentina and Uruguay are called "pampas". The temperate grasslands of Hungary are called "puszta". The grasslands of South Africa are called "veldts" while those of North America are called "prairies". The most important among these are prairies and steppes.

Grasses, flowers and soils

Like in the tropical grasslands, the vegetation of temperate grasslands is dominated by perennial grasses and forbs. The major species of grass are the buffalo grass, purple needlegrass, blue grama, ryegrass, foxtail, etc. Wildflowers grow alongside. The major species of flowers are sunflowers, wild indigos, asters, clovers and blazing stars.

The grass roots are branched and spread deep into the soil. The upper layers of soil are rich in nutrients and extremely fertile. As the roots of the grasses are fixed deep into the soil, they are protected from fires and grazing animals. However, shrubs and other small plants do not have this same protection and often die out quickly.

Violet asters and blazing stars.

Tall-grass prairie of the Midewin and short-grass prairie of the Llano Estacado.

Tall or short

The height of grasses in a grassland depends upon the amount of rainfall and water it receives. For example, the grasses in the prairies grow to be about 6 feet as they receive an annual rainfall of 25-75 cm. Steppes have short grasses as they receive an annual rainfall of 25-50 cm.

Even within the prairies, there are short-grass and tall-grass prairies. The area that receives an annual rainfall below 40 cm is called "short-grass prairie" while the one that receives above 40 cm is called "tall-grass prairie".

FUN FACT

Temperate grasslands have a long history of terrible fires that were caused by human activity or by lightning. These fires can spread to 600 feet in just a few minutes.

Pamperos

Buenos Aires of the Pampas experiences periodic storms known as "pamperos". They are caused when the cool winds coming from the southern side of the pampas join the warm air travelling from the northern tropical climates. These storms consist of strong ferocious gales and heavy rains.

Distribution of Snow

About 23 per cent of Earth's surface is covered by a layer of snow. During winter, this cover increases to 40 per cent. On an average, about 47 million km^2 is covered by snow per year. 98 per cent is concentrated in the Northern Hemisphere. It might last for a short time or lie on the surface permanently (or as permanent as can be on our ever-changing Earth).

Wet bulb temperature

There is a wet bulb thermometer that measures the temperature of air that is close to the ground. To understand if the precipitation will form snow and fall to the ground as snow without melting, we must look at the wet bulb thermometer. The temperature it displays must be below 0 °C.

It is measured by taking a thermometer that has a small sock-like material wrapped around its bulb. This thermometer is swung into the air in a circular manner. The wet bulb temperature does not take into account the temperature of the air as even if the air has a temperature slightly above 0 °C, the snow will fall because of the negative degrees of ground air temperature.

The Perito Moreno glacier in Argentina is the third largest glacier in the world.

Snow and its forms

Snow is precipitation that falls on Earth's surface in places where the temperature is below 0 °C. Water vapour in the air directly hardens into crystals of ice, which then form interlaced patterns with other crystals to form snowflakes. They may also form unusual clusters of various shapes.

If the ground temperature is also below 0 °C, these crystals and flakes of snow can build up and cover the surface in a white blanket of snow. Earth's surface is covered by freezing seas, lakes, rivers, sheets of ice, snow, floating ice, glaciers and ice caps that cover the freezing ground.

Where does it snow?

There is snowfall in the equator but only in high altitudes such as the peaks of high mountains. The mountains that have snow have an elevation of about 16,000 feet. Otherwise, snowfall occurs at sea level only between 35° N and 35° S. This mostly takes place at the extreme ends of the Northern and Southern Hemispheres.

Annually, Russia, Greenland, Europe and North America receive the most amount of snow. Antarctica mainly experiences snowfall during the winter. During the winter, the tall mountains of South America and New Zealand receive snow.

It is said that no two snowflakes have the same pattern.

Rivers of Ice

Glaciers are a product of snow. When snow accumulates at one place for a long time, it hardens into a thick, solid block of ice. This is heavy and sometimes huge. Due to its weight and gravity, it begins to move on land. The glaciers on a valley move downwards, while those on a flatter land surface move away in any direction. They are also called "Ice Rivers".

Pressure melting

The name "glacier" is derived from the French word "glace" which means "ice". Glaciers are formed when snowfall accumulates and buries the present layer of snow on the surface. The snowflakes within this layer slowly change into granules of snow, then harden and compact into solids. These hardened granules then recrystallise to form the hard ice of a glacier. This entire process is called "pressure melting".

A melting glacier.

Cryosphere

The cryosphere, like the biosphere and ecosystem, is a system of Earth that comprises the frozen water part and those areas whose temperatures remain below the freezing point of water (0 °C). Glaciers make up a large part of the cryosphere.

Glaciation

Glaciation is the process by which glaciers and glacial landforms are formed and shaped. Glaciations occur at high altitudes or elevations at Earth's poles. Over time, the average temperature at these places has dropped. These drops in temperature have occurred due to the change in seasons caused by Earth's orbit and the tilt of its axis. This causes a variation in the amount of solar radiation received by Earth. This also varies due to the slight wobbling Earth experiences at its axis.

Reducing glacial cover

Even though 10 per cent of Earth's surface is covered by glaciers and glacial ice, all of it is concentrated in the Arctic and Antarctic. About 20,000 years ago, nearly 30 per cent of Earth's surface was covered by glaciers. According to geological evidence, almost all of Canada and most of North America were covered in glacial matter. This change in the glacial cover is a result of the glaciation that took place nearly 18,000 years ago.

Earth is slowly losing its glacial cover.

TYPES OF GLACIERS

Glacial landscapes are affected by the glaciation processes of erosion, weathering, deposition and transportation (the movement of glaciers). Glaciers are primarily classified upon their location, then structure and size. The glaciers present on Earth today can be classified into two types—Alpine glaciers and continental glaciers (ice sheets).

Glaciers that are formed on the sides of mountains are called "Alpine glaciers". These glaciers move down the valleys of the mountains. There are different types of Alpine glaciers:

Piedmont glaciers: Sometimes, two glaciers meet at the base of the valley and begin to combine and form a new glacier. This glacier is called, "piedmont glacier".

Tidewater glacier: The piedmont glacier continues to move. On its path, if it flows into seawater, it is called, "tidewater glacier".

Cirque glacier: These glaciers are formed when snow accumulates at the head of the valley, in its basin (which has a semi-circular shape) and forms hard glacial ice.

Valley glacier: As snow continues to accumulate over a cirque glacier, it grows larger and overflows the valley. It begins to move downhill. This is a "valley glacier".

Ice caps: These are formed when valleys of a mountain range are completely covered by glaciers. These glaciers slowly cover the entire mountain range as "ice caps".

Continental glaciers

Continental glaciers are some of the largest on Earth. They are formed flatlands and mountains. They begin to flow away from central glacial areas. Ice sheets make up about 95 per cent of Earth's total glacial cover, most being located on Greenland and Antarctica. Some are classified as temperate glaciers, with temperatures close to melting points. They are also classified as polar glaciers.

Structure of a glacier

As snow accumulates and hardens, it forms a matter called "firn". These are the granules that slowly compact and crystallise into glacial ice. Firn is formed at the head of the glacier where snow accumulates. This part is called the "zone of accumulation". The part that slowly melts or evaporates into icebergs is the "zone of ablation". It is at the foot of a glacier. The part that separates these zones is called the "equilibrium line".

An iceberg in Antarctica.

FLOATING ICE

Icebergs are products of glaciers. They are formed by a process called "calving". By this process, chunks of ice break from a moving glacier and drop into the nearby water. The chunks of ice always break at the end or foot of a glacier as this portion is more prone to cracking due to the forward movement of glaciers.

Icebergs

Icebergs were made infamous in 1912 by the sinking of a ship named "Titanic". These are humungous blocks of ice that were once a part of a large glacier. These blocks of ice broke away by the process of calving. Usually, an iceberg is formed from a tidewater glacier, when the foot of this glacier meets the seawater.

What are icebergs made of?

Icebergs float in oceans. About 90 per cent of their structure is hidden under the surface of water. Icebergs are made of freshwater that is frozen over time and forms a hard ice structure. They float on the saltwater of the ocean.

Source of an iceberg

The source of an iceberg can be traced back easily based on the direction in which it is flowing. The icebergs of the Northern Hemisphere are mostly formed by the glaciers in Greenland. From here, they float to the south towards North Atlantic Ocean. The icebergs floating away from the continent of Antarctica are formed by the glaciers here.

Types of icebergs

Icebergs come in various sizes. The ones that are less than 16 feet long and greater than 3 feet are called "bergy bits". Icebergs that are smaller than bergy bits are called "growlers". There are some icebergs that are larger than the island of Sicily. Only about 12 per cent of an iceberg is visible above the surface of water. A group of icebergs that are no more than 6 feet in length is called "brash ice". An iceberg can also be formed when it breaks away from an ice shelf. This is called "tabular berg" as it has a flat upper surface.

Growlers and bergy bits that have broken off from the main iceberg.

WILD IN THE SNOW

The wildlife of the Polar Regions (that is the Arctic and the Antarctic) is exposed to one of the harshest climates on Earth. Yet there are many species of animals that live comfortably in this region.

Caribou.

King penguin couple.

Animals of the Antarctic

Antarctica is like an island continent that is surrounded by sea. There is a rich marine life present in the sea around the Antarctic continent. There is an abundance of plankton in the sea which allows the marine life to flourish. Fishes and shrimp (called "krill") are some examples of marine life. These are the food of birds like skuas and penguins. There are also sea animals like whales and seas that live in the water. In fact, there are eight species of whales here.

Animals of the Arctic

Caribou, a type of reindeer, is the most popular and most common animal of the Arctic. Besides it, there are other species of reindeer, the musk ox and collared lemming (a type of rodent). Migratory birds such as geese and ducks of different species come to the Arctic to rest and eat. The arctic fox, weasel and brown bear are the carnivorous animals of the arctic. The water is home to seals which are preyed upon by polar bears. Besides seals, the water also has whales, walruses and narwhals along with other microscopic aquatic animals.

Most large animals of the Arctic live here during the summer and feed on the grass. However, during the winter they migrate to the south to feed upon lichens that live upon the grass and trees there.

Adaptations of the animals

Fishes and other aquatic animals have adapted themselves to be comfortable in all weather. Larger aquatic animals such as whales and seals have a layer of blubber, which is fat, right under their skin. This helps keep them warm. Though penguins are amphibians that can live on land and water, they too have a layer of blubber to keep them warm.

Most of the mammals and birds of this region are warm-blooded animals that need to migrate or hibernate during the colder climate to survive. Polar bears and other large animals have a thick coat of fur upon their skin that keeps them warm.

Polar bears can also swim in water in order to find food.

A LAND OF SAND

Deserts are places whose annual precipitation is less than 25-50 cm. There are many types of deserts. Two of these are the subtropical deserts, which have a hot climate and the temperate deserts which have a cold climate. About one-fifth of Earth's surface is covered by desert regions.

Distribution of deserts

Deserts occur in places that experience low precipitation and rainfall. Most deserts occur from the latitudes of 30° N and 30° S, away from the tropical climate. This region receives warm air from the equator which falls as cool, dry air as it lost its water vapour over the equator. Deserts occur in certain places due to the lack of moisture in the rain clouds.

Rain shadow effect

Some deserts are found by the mountain ranges. They are formed by the "rain shadow effect". The air that travels over a mountain range slowly cools and loses its moisture. This causes rainfall or snowfall.

As the air travels to the opposite end of the mountain, it begins to warm and becomes able to hold more moisture. This area experiences little or no rainfall, thus forming a desert. The deserts of Australia were formed by the rain shadow effect.

A diagram showing the rain shadow effect over the Sierra Nevada.

Diverting rain clouds

Deserts occur at places that experience high pressure. This is the reason that rain clouds are turned away from this region. Deserts are the hottest at noon as the Sun is positioned directly above the Tropic of Cancer or Tropic of Capricorn at noon. The Southern Hemisphere has more deserts than the Northern Hemisphere for these reasons.

The common view of deserts is that it has a hot climate. However, some deserts such as the Atacama Desert in Chile, South America and the Kalahari Desert of Africa were actually formed by the cold oceanic currents that turn away the rain clouds coming from the coasts.

Distance from the ocean

The Gobi Desert is the result of its great distance from the ocean. The moisture present in the cold winds blowing from the Pacific Ocean is lost by the time it reaches this region. Even the little moisture coming from the rain clouds from the Indian Ocean is spent in the Himalayas. As a result, the land-locked Gobi Desert is formed.

LIFE IN THE DESERT

Deserts receive very little rainfall. In most deserts, it rains for an average of 20 days in a year. There are some deserts which do not receive rainfall for decades together. The Cochones Desert in Chile, for example, did not receive rainfall from 1919 to 1964. This is why, all deserts are classified as "dry lands".

Vegetations on desert.

Rainfall

The land of deserts (except Polar Deserts) is extremely hot as the Sun's rays fall directly upon it. For the deserts closer to the equator, the Sun might be overhead causing even more increase in the temperature. As a result, deserts do not have a strong enough atmosphere to protect the land from radiant energy.

As a result of this low rainfall, the rate of evaporation is very high. This means that the rainwater is sometimes evaporated even before it touches the land. The land in the interior of the Sahara Desert as well as the Atacama Desert receives an annual rainfall of 1.5 cm. Otherwise, the average annual rainfall in a desert is 28 cm.

This image shows a sand desert.

FUN FACT
Did you know that the desert plays tricks on people? Sometimes, people see a pool of cool, refreshing water in the distance. But when they go closer, it disappears. Actually, this pool of water never existed. It is an optical illusion called "mirage".

An oasis.

Oasis

Have you heard of an oasis? It is another source of water in the deserts. When underground water comes to the surface as a spring, it sometimes helps create a green patch. This patch is called "oasis" or "cienega". The Sahara Desert itself has about 90 oases. Desert settlements, animals and plants of most desert areas are based around these oases.

Subtropical dry. desert.

Climate of the subtropical and dry desert

As there is very little humidity in the desert air, the temperature and weather can change suddenly and drastically. During the morning, the ground in a desert receives lots of radiation from the Sun (50° C). During the night, it loses almost all of its heat so that the temperatures at night are freezing (about -18 °C).

Climate in the coastal desert

The coastal deserts experience extremely warm and long summers. The average summer temperature in the deserts is 13-24° C. These are followed by cool and mild temperature in the winter. The temperature can drop to 5° C during winter. The annual rainfall here is about 8-13 cm with an annual precipitation of 5-37 cm.

Climate of the Polar desert

Cold deserts experience a completely different climate. In most places, instead of rainfall, the precipitation falls to the ground as snow. So, the average temperatures range from -2 to -4 °C throughout the year, except during summer when the average temperature is 21-26 °C.

This image shows a polar desert which is completely covered by snow.

Sources of water

Though there is very little rainfall in a desert, it is the major source of water for the plants, animals and people living here. Whatever water is received is carefully stored by the people of the desert. Groundwater from aquifers (a layer of rock or soil near the surface) is another source of water for the people. This water comes from rain or snow which can remain in the ground for hundreds of years.

The price of water

In some deserts, people recognise the groundwater areas or aquifers and drill holes in the ground to get to the water. This water is used for bathing, drinking, agriculture and other purposes. People face water shortage if they use this water faster than it is refilled.

Types of soils

All deserts, except cold deserts, have grainy, rocky and coarse soil. They do not absorb much water and do not undergo much chemical weathering. Physical weathering or wind erosion is common in deserts with lots of sand. Thin, light sand blows elsewhere while heavier rocks and finer particles settle on the soil. Some deserts contain salt. The soil in cold deserts is salty but heavier. It contains silt. Some soils are spongy and leech out the salt content.

LANDFORMS OF THE DESERT

Most people, when they think of the desert, think of sand. But sand covers only one-fifth of the total deserts on Earth. Deserts have some special landforms that are unique only to them. Rolling sand dunes are one of the most common and fascinating landforms of the desert.

Sand dunes

Basically, a sand dune is a large mound of sand. Sand dunes are formed when strong winds blow sand from one place and let it accumulate at another. It is a temporary structure whose size can increase or decrease by the next strong wave of wind. Sand dunes are also found in sandy beaches, but in much smaller sizes. In fact, "true dunes of the desert", as they are called, are differentiated from sand dunes in beaches and barren lands by their size.

Sand dunes of the Great Sand Dunes National Park and Preserve.

Playa

Playa (read as ply-uh), is a very uncommon sight in a desert. A playa is formed when precipitation falls to the land as rain and collects in low-lying places instead of evaporating or collecting underground. This water forms a temporary lake which later evaporates or is absorbed by the land. As it evaporates, it leaves behind sediments that move along the desert floor, carried forward by the evaporating water.

This is called "playa". If the water remains back to form a small body of water, it is called "playa lake". The Great Salt Lake in Utah and the Dead Sea in Israel are permanent playa lakes.

Structure of a sand dune

Sand dunes have a windward side. It is the side where the wind is most active, pushing particles of sand upward and affecting the overlying particles. Sand dunes also have a slipface side which is the side opposite to the windward side. The wind from the windward side does not reach here, so the sand is smooth and stable. A dune field is a place that has many sand dunes.

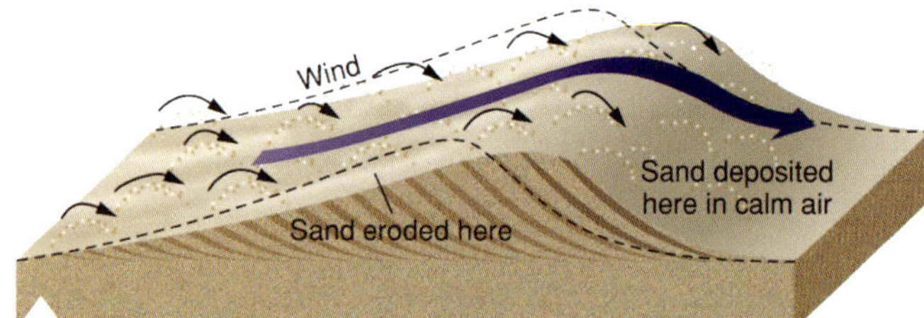

A diagram showing the structure of a sand dune.

Tallest sand dune

The Sechura Desert in Peru has the tallest sand dune in the world. Its name is Cerro Blanco and it is 3,860 feet tall!

The Great Salt Lake in Utah.